BLAST OFF! THE SCIENCE OF SPACE

SCIENCE FOR ROCKETING INTO SPACE

Mark Thompson

Please visit our website, www.garethstevens.com. For a free color catalog of all our high-quality books, call toll free 1-800-542-2595 or fax 1-877-542-2596.

Cataloging-in-Publication Data

Names: Thompson, Mark.
Title: Science for rocketing into space / Mark Thompson.
Description: New York : Gareth Stevens Publishing, 2024. |
Series: Blast off!: the science of space | Includes glossary and index.
Identifiers: ISBN 9781538287859 (pbk.) | ISBN 9781538287866 (library bound) | ISBN 9781538287873 (ebook)
Subjects: LCSH: Astronautics--Juvenile literature. | Astronautics--Experiments--Juvenile literature. | Space vehicles--Juvenile literature. | Outer space--Exploration--Juvenile literature.
Classification: LCC TL793.T466 2024 | DDC 629.409--dc23

Published in 2024 by
Gareth Stevens Publishing
2544 Clinton St.
Buffalo, NY 14224

First published in Great Britain in 2019 by Wayland

Editor: Amy Pimperton
Design and illustration: Collaborate

Note: In preparation of this book, all due care has been exercised with regard to the instructions, activities and techniques depicted. The publishers regret that they can accept no liability for any loss or injury sustained. Always get adult supervision and follow manufacturers' advice when using electric and battery-powered appliances.

Printed in the United States of America

CPSIA compliance information: Batch #CSGS24: For further information contact Gareth Stevens at 1-800-542-2595.

CONTENTS

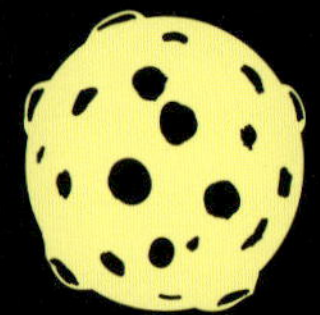

REACH FOR THE STARS

Do you think that you can jump high enough so that you can reach the moon? Give it a try now, jump as high as you can and see if you can make it. If you are a great jumper, you might be able to jump as high as a few feet, but you will probably not get much higher than that.

The force of gravity keeps us firmly stuck to Earth's surface, so if you want to get into space, then you are going to need some help.

FAR-OUT IDEAS!

What do you think you could use? You could use a giant rubber band, a massive spring, or maybe even shoot yourself out of a cannon. These ideas might get you a few more feet, but to get into space you are going to need something else—a rocket.

EARLY ROCKETS

The first rockets were made hundreds of years ago by the Chinese and Babylonians (the Babylonians were people of a region in what is now Iraq). They filled bamboo sticks with explosive powder and then threw them onto a fire to celebrate some exciting occasion. The bamboo sticks would give off a loud CRACK and fly off in all directions. This was very dangerous and definitely not something to try at home!

UP IN SMOKE

According to an ancient story, one brave Chinese emperor, called Wan Hu, decided to become the first space traveler by strapping 47 of these rockets to a chair!

He sat on the chair in his finest robes while the rockets were lit. There was a massive bang and clouds of smoke, and he was never seen again! Maybe Wan Hu made it into space and never came back.

AWESOME ENGINEERING

Rockets today are far safer than Wan Hu's chair, and his chair would probably not help us get into space.

So we can see how rockets send humans safely into space, we are going to look at how rockets work, how they lift off, how they can be made to fly in straight lines, their shape, and what it would feel like to be inside a spacecraft floating around in weightlessness.

This book is full of fun experiments and investigations that explore how rockets work.

ESCAPE GRAVITY

To get into space, a rocket has to overcome the pull of Earth's gravity. It does this by traveling at around 25,031 miles (40,284 km) per hour. Larger planets, such as Jupiter, usually have a stronger pull of gravity, which means a rocket is heavier there and must travel faster to overcome gravity. To explore gravity on Jupiter, we need to compare the weight of something on Earth with how much it would weigh on Jupiter.

YOU WILL NEED:

- two identical empty jam jars
- some sand
- a cup
- scales
- a notebook and pencil

1 Take one jam jar and put a cup of sand in it.

2 Place the jam jar on the scales. Make a note of its weight.

SCIENCE FACT

Everything in the universe is made of matter: a table, yourself, the sun and moon. The amount of matter in something is called its mass. The more mass something has, the stronger its gravitational pull. Anything made of matter pulls everything else made of matter toward it. Sometimes this pull is small so we don't notice it. Bigger gravitational pulls are more obvious, such as a ball being pulled to the ground by Earth's gravity.

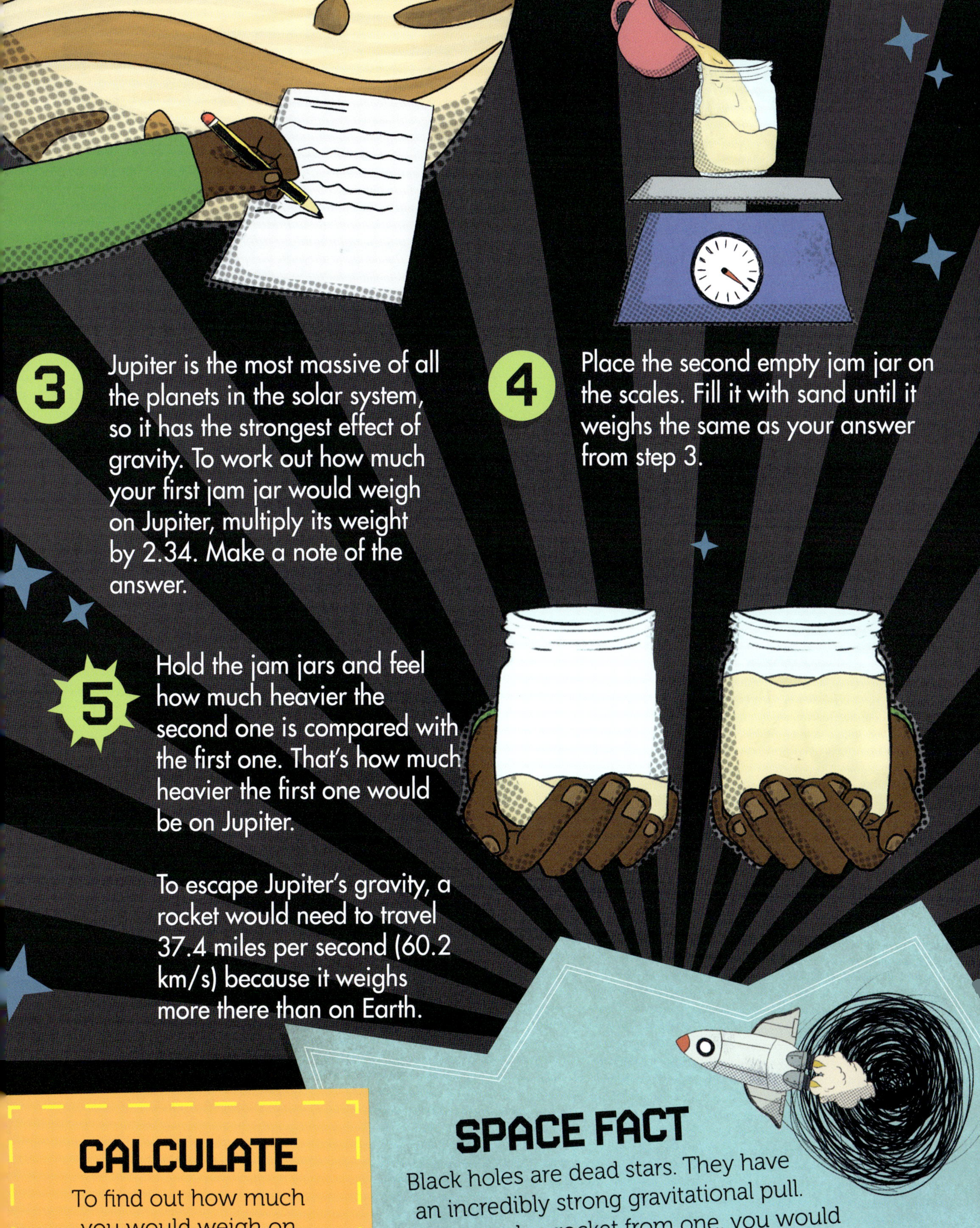

3 Jupiter is the most massive of all the planets in the solar system, so it has the strongest effect of gravity. To work out how much your first jam jar would weigh on Jupiter, multiply its weight by 2.34. Make a note of the answer.

4 Place the second empty jam jar on the scales. Fill it with sand until it weighs the same as your answer from step 3.

5 Hold the jam jars and feel how much heavier the second one is compared with the first one. That's how much heavier the first one would be on Jupiter.

To escape Jupiter's gravity, a rocket would need to travel 37.4 miles per second (60.2 km/s) because it weighs more there than on Earth.

CALCULATE

To find out how much you would weigh on Jupiter, multiply your weight by 2.34.

SPACE FACT

Black holes are dead stars. They have an incredibly strong gravitational pull. To launch a rocket from one, you would need to travel faster than the speed of light—186,000 miles per second (300,000 km/s)!

OVERCOME INERTIA ... WITH AN EGG

When a rocket sits on its launch pad, it has something called inertia. A rocket shooting through space also has inertia. Inertia describes how something does not want to change what it is doing. In the case of a rocket on a launch pad, its engines are off, so it doesn't want to move. If it is zooming through space, it wants to continue zooming through space. Before we can launch a rocket into space, we must overcome its inertia. You can explore inertia with an egg!

YOU WILL NEED:

- a plastic beaker
- some water
- a shallow tray
- a short cardboard tube
- a fresh egg

RED ALERT!
This could get messy, so do it outside.

1 Fill the plastic beaker about three-quarters full of water.

2 Place the shallow tray on top of the beaker. Place the cardboard tube on top of the tray so that it is directly above the beaker.

3 Carefully place the egg on top of the cardboard tube. Notice what the egg is doing! It's doing nothing sitting on top of the tube. It has inertia, which means it does not want to start moving.

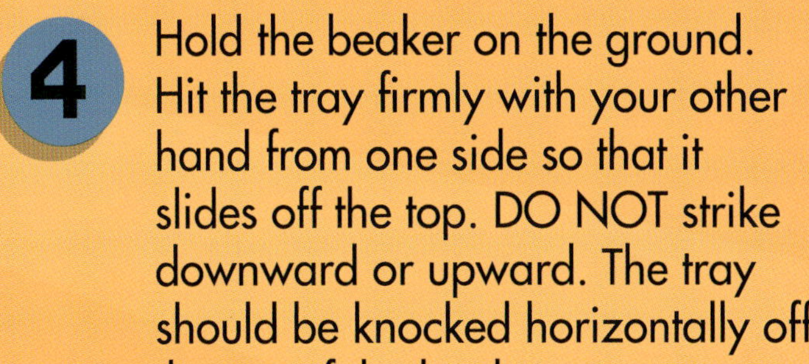

4 Hold the beaker on the ground. Hit the tray firmly with your other hand from one side so that it slides off the top. DO NOT strike downward or upward. The tray should be knocked horizontally off the top of the beaker.

5 The lip of the tray will knock the tube out from under the egg. The egg, which has inertia, resists any movement and, for a tiny fraction of a second, does nothing. Gravity soon overcomes the egg's inertia, and the egg drops into the water.

SPACE FACT

We get high tides because of the pull of gravity from the moon. One high tide lies on the side of Earth closest to the moon. On the opposite side, another high tide occurs. This high tide is partly due to inertia. As Earth spins at around 1,000 miles per hour (1,609 km/h), the inertia of the water trying not to move causes the high tide.

EXPLORE EPIC EXOTHERMIC ERUPTIONS

For a rocket to get into space, it needs something to push it. The pushing force comes from the explosive energy created by a chemical reaction between liquid hydrogen and liquid oxygen. This type of chemical reaction is exothermic, which means it gives off lots and lots of energy. Hydrogen is very dangerous though, so to explore chemical reactions we are going to use hydrogen peroxide to create an eruption of foam.

YOU WILL NEED:

- a mixing bowl and spoon
- 3 tablespoons (44 ml) of water
- 4 teaspoons of bakers' yeast
- a clean, empty two-liter soda bottle
- a tray (optional)
- safety goggles
- a measuring cup
- hydrogen peroxide, 9% strength, (available from pharmacies)
- liquid dish soap
- food coloring (optional)
- a small funnel (optional)

1 In a bowl, mix 3 tablespoons (44 ml) of warm water with 4 level teaspoons of yeast until it is a thick liquid.

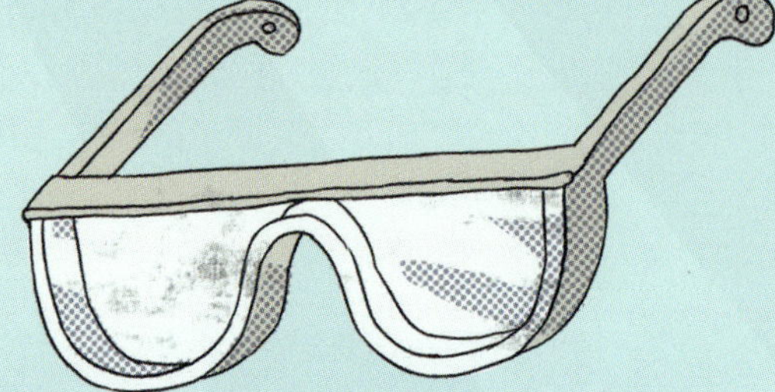

2 Place the soda bottle on a large tray. If you don't have one, place it on the ground outside.

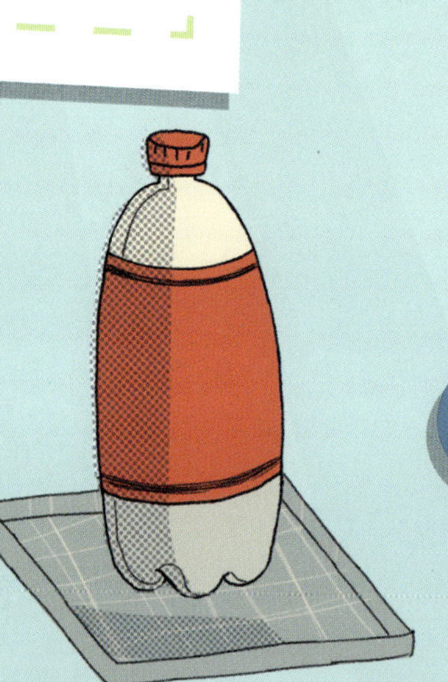

3 Put on your safety goggles. DO NOT put your face over the bottle as you perform this experiment.

4

Pour about 1/2 cup (about 120 ml) of hydrogen peroxide into the soda bottle.

RED ALERT!

Ask an adult to help you handle hydrogen peroxide. If it gets into your eyes or onto your skin, wash it off with water. Never swallow it!

5

Add a good squirt of dish soap. You could add some food coloring at this stage too if you want colorful foam.

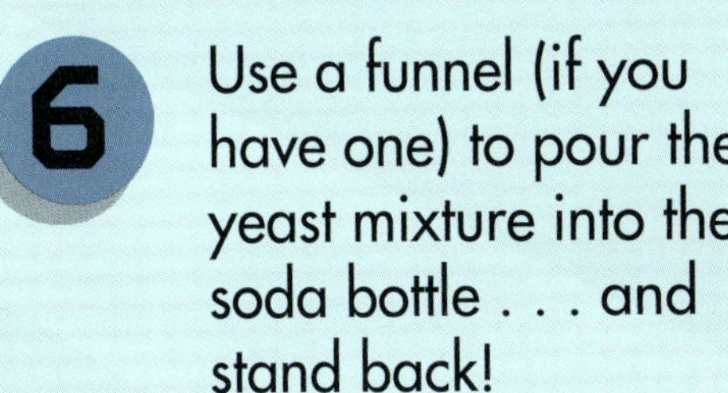

6

Use a funnel (if you have one) to pour the yeast mixture into the soda bottle . . . and stand back!

SCIENCE FACT

Hydrogen peroxide contains hydrogen and oxygen. The yeast causes a chemical reaction that breaks apart the hydrogen peroxide to form oxygen and water. The dish soap traps the oxygen, creating loads of little bubbles. Notice how the bottle feels warm to the touch; the chemical reaction created heat, too, in an exothermic reaction. The foam and liquid are all safe to wash down the sink.

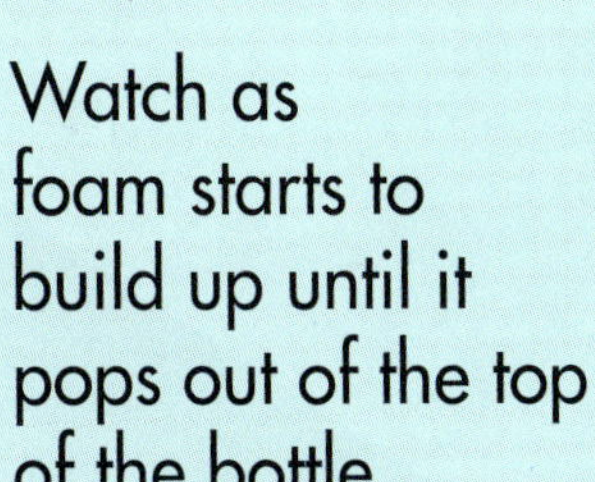

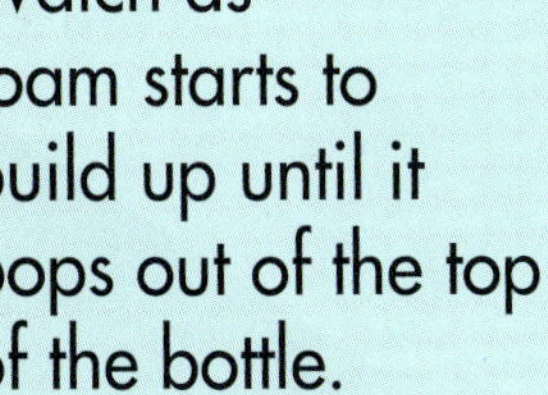

7

Watch as foam starts to build up until it pops out of the top of the bottle.

BALLOON TO THE MOON

Watching a rocket roar off a launch pad is an amazing sight. A rocket on a launch pad is pulled down to Earth by gravity. As soon as the rocket fires its engines, they create an unbalanced pushing force that is stronger than the force of gravity, so the rocket shoots upward.

We measure force in Newtons. The engines on the Saturn V rocket that sent Neil Armstrong (1930–2012) to the moon produced 33,400,000 Newtons! Even if you don't have a Saturn V, you can still explore forces with a balloon rocket!

YOU WILL NEED:

- a straw
- scissors
- a long piece of string
- a balloon
- sticky tape

1 Cut the straw into a straight piece about 2.5 inches (6 cm) in length.

2.5 in

SCIENCE FACT

Newtons are named after the scientist Sir Isaac Newton (1642–1727). His third law of motion says: "For every action there is an equal and opposite reaction." Think of two friends, each standing on their own skateboard. If one friend gently pushes the other, then the friend who was pushed (the action) will move away, but the friend doing the pushing will also move away (the equal and opposite reaction).

2 Thread the string through the straw.

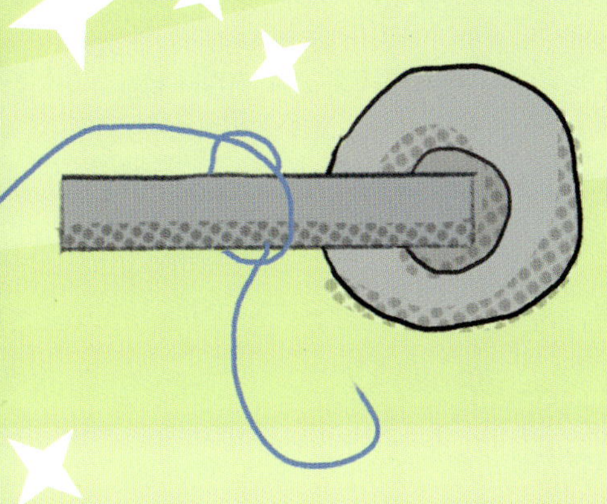

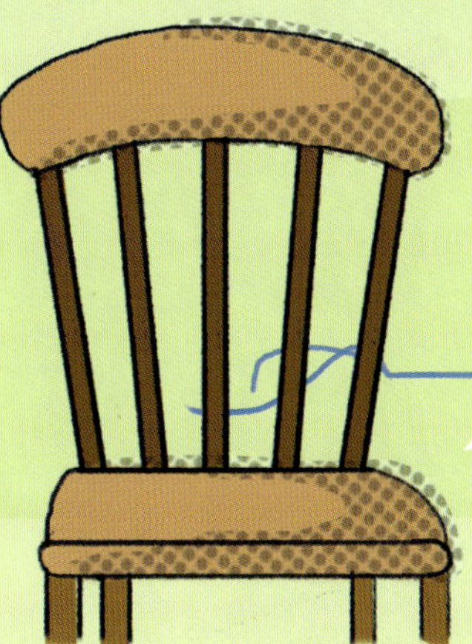

3

Tie one end of the string to a door handle or some other stable point that is easy to reach.

4

Pull the string tight and tie the other end to another point, such as a chair. Check that the straw slides along the string easily.

5

Blow up the balloon, but do not tie a knot in it. Instead, hold the end of the balloon tightly so that the air can't escape.

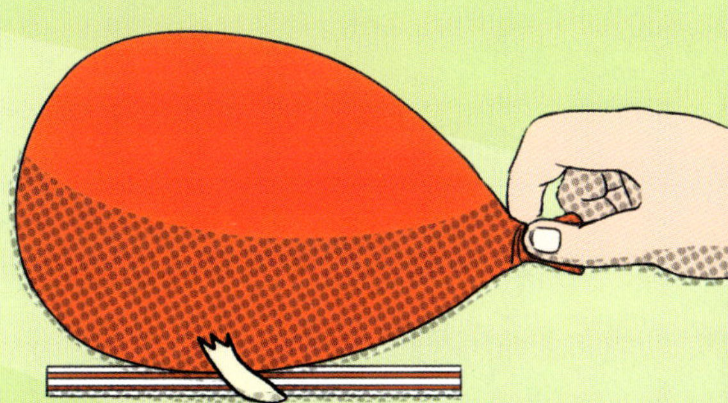

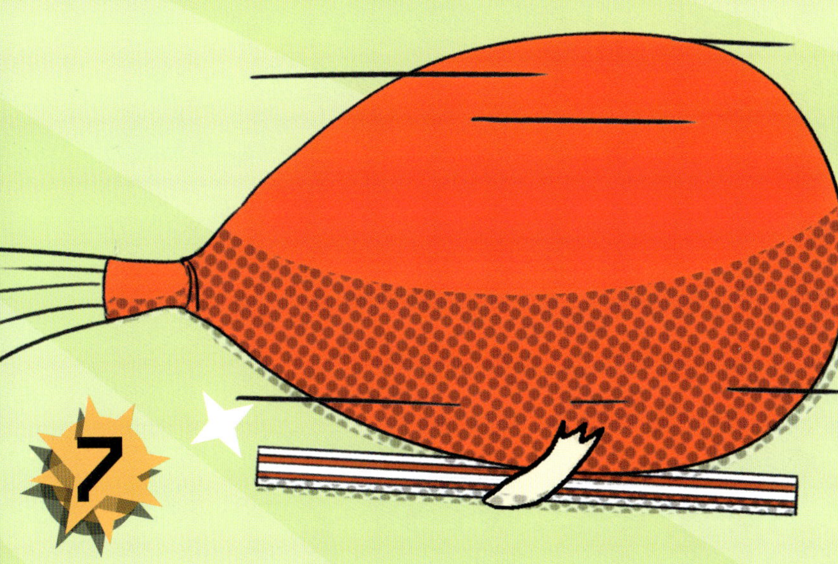

6

Ask a friend to stick the balloon to the straw with sticky tape while you are holding the air in the balloon.

7

Pull the balloon back to the end of the string so that the neck of the balloon is closest to one end of the string. Now the fun part! Let go of the balloon and watch as Newton's third law of motion pushes the balloon along the string, just like a real rocket.

SPACE FACT

A Saturn V rocket weighed 6.2 million pounds (2.8 million kg)—the same as 400 elephants!

LOWER THE CENTER OF GRAVITY

An object's center of gravity is a point where all of its weight is concentrated and the object balances perfectly. An object can be made more stable and less likely to fall over by lowering its center of gravity. A rocket on a launch pad is stable because its center of gravity is concentrated above its base.

The position of a rocket's center of gravity changes during flight as fuel gets used up and bits of the rocket fall away. Astronauts need to know where the rocket's center of gravity is at all times to ensure the rocket is stable as it flies. In this fun experiment, we play around with the center of gravity of a pencil.

YOU WILL NEED:

- a pencil (sharpened)
- two pipe cleaners or pieces of garden wire about 6 inches (15 cm) long
- two clothespins

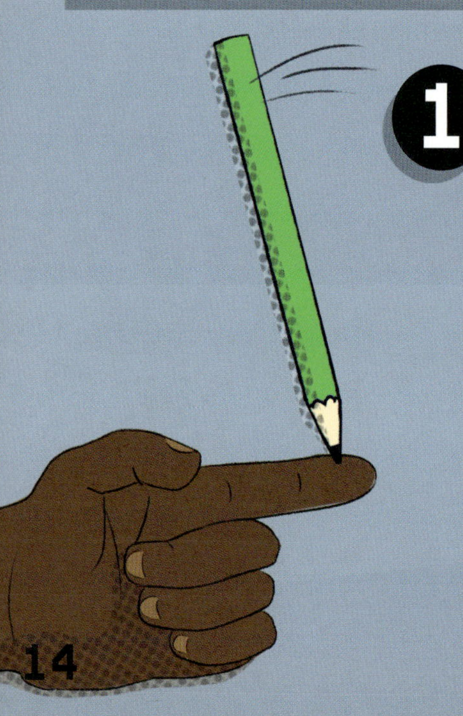

1. First, try to balance the pencil with its point on your finger. You won't be able to do it because the center of gravity of the pencil is too high. At the moment, it is about halfway up the length of the pencil.

2. Take a pipe cleaner, or garden wire, and wind one end around the pencil, about 0.5 inch (1 cm) above the point.

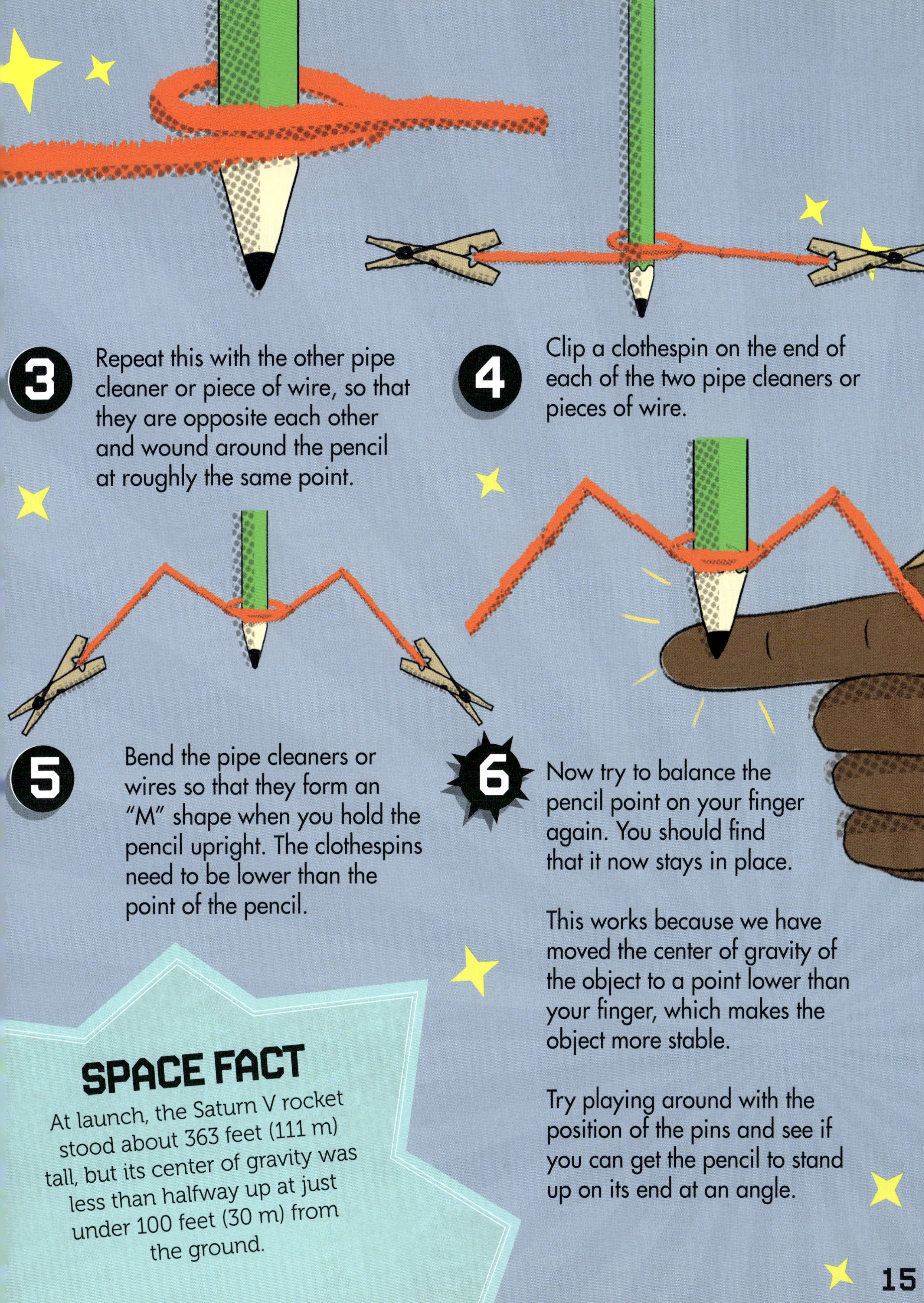

3 Repeat this with the other pipe cleaner or piece of wire, so that they are opposite each other and wound around the pencil at roughly the same point.

4 Clip a clothespin on the end of each of the two pipe cleaners or pieces of wire.

5 Bend the pipe cleaners or wires so that they form an "M" shape when you hold the pencil upright. The clothespins need to be lower than the point of the pencil.

6 Now try to balance the pencil point on your finger again. You should find that it now stays in place.

This works because we have moved the center of gravity of the object to a point lower than your finger, which makes the object more stable.

Try playing around with the position of the pins and see if you can get the pencil to stand up on its end at an angle.

SPACE FACT

At launch, the Saturn V rocket stood about 363 feet (111 m) tall, but its center of gravity was less than halfway up at just under 100 feet (30 m) from the ground.

BLAST OFF ... WITH A CHEMICAL REACTION

Rockets are driven by powerful reactions between chemicals, such as liquid oxygen and liquid hydrogen (see pages 10–11). A chemical reaction is when one set of chemical substances is changed into another.

In this case, hydrogen and oxygen are changed into H_2O—water! The reaction creates loads of energy in the form of steam, which increases the pressure inside the rocket engine, pushing the rocket up into space. You can create the same effect with a film canister and an antacid tablet.

YOU WILL NEED:

- an antacid table— ask an adult for one (available from pharmacies)
- a film canister (these can be bought online or from photo processing shops—white ones work best)
- some water
- a stopwatch or wristwatch with a second hand

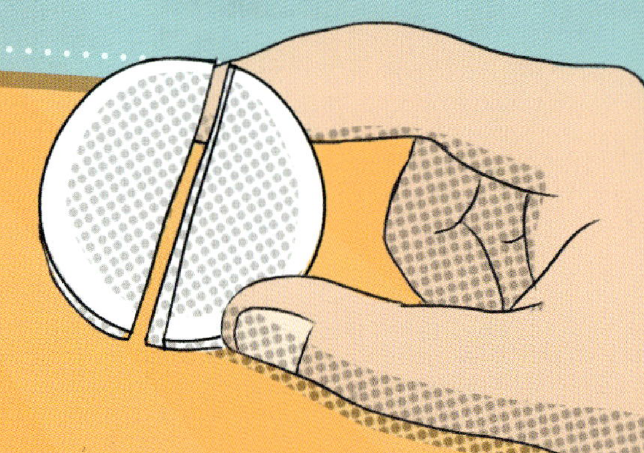

1 Prepare for your launch by breaking an antacid tablet in half.

2 Remove the lid from the film canister. Carefully pour in a little water until the film canister is about a quarter full.

3 Take the film canister, lid, and antacid tablet outside.

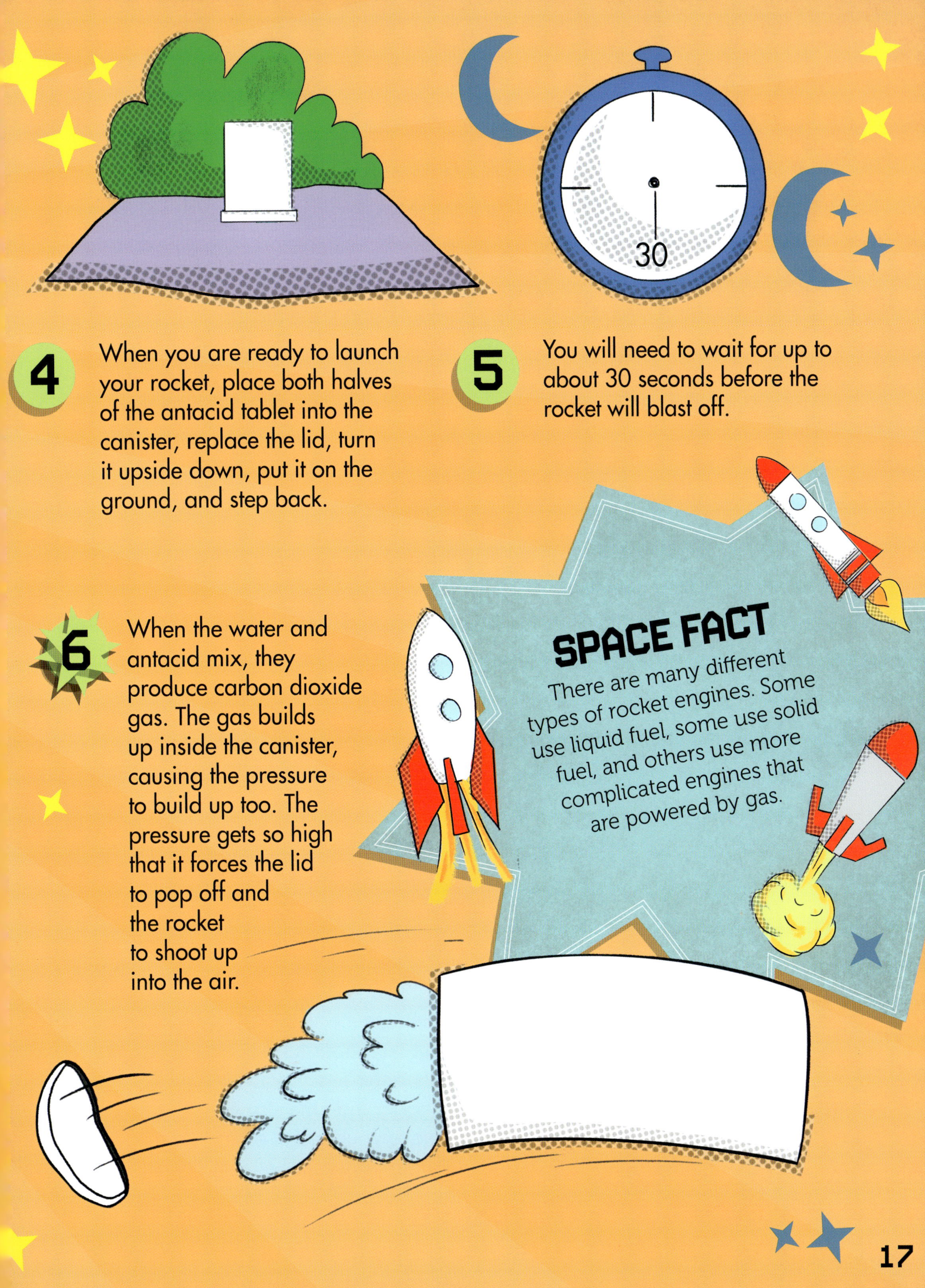

4 When you are ready to launch your rocket, place both halves of the antacid tablet into the canister, replace the lid, turn it upside down, put it on the ground, and step back.

5 You will need to wait for up to about 30 seconds before the rocket will blast off.

6 When the water and antacid mix, they produce carbon dioxide gas. The gas builds up inside the canister, causing the pressure to build up too. The pressure gets so high that it forces the lid to pop off and the rocket to shoot up into the air.

SPACE FACT

There are many different types of rocket engines. Some use liquid fuel, some use solid fuel, and others use more complicated engines that are powered by gas.

LAUNCH A STRAW ROCKET ... WITH PUFF POWER

Why are rockets rocket-shaped? Everything, including air, is made up of tiny particles we cannot see, called molecules. Air molecules hit the rocket and slow it down as it tries to travel through them.

We call this effect drag, so rockets are shaped to cut through the air and hit as few air molecules as possible. This is done by designing rockets with a small surface area and an aerodynamic shape. In this activity, see how a rocket's design helps it fly.

YOU WILL NEED:

- a sheet of printer paper
- scissors
- a straw
- sticky tape
- a small sheet of colored paper

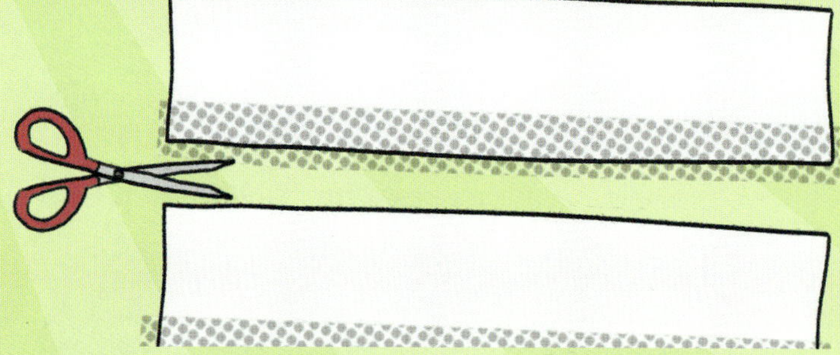

1. Cut the sheet of paper in half lengthways.

2. Roll one half lengthways around the straw, making sure it is not too tight. Fix it in place with sticky tape to make a tube.

3. Remove the straw and cut the paper tube so it is about 1 inch (2.5 cm) shorter than the straw. To make your rocket a more streamlined shape, neatly fold over the top, and secure it with tape.

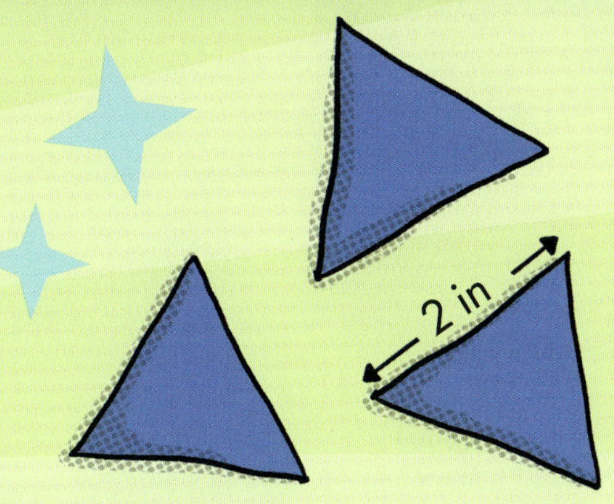

4 Cut out three triangles from the colored paper. They should be about 2 inches (5 cm) along each side.

5 To help your rocket balance, tape the triangles to the bottom of the paper tube, so that they are equally spaced around it.

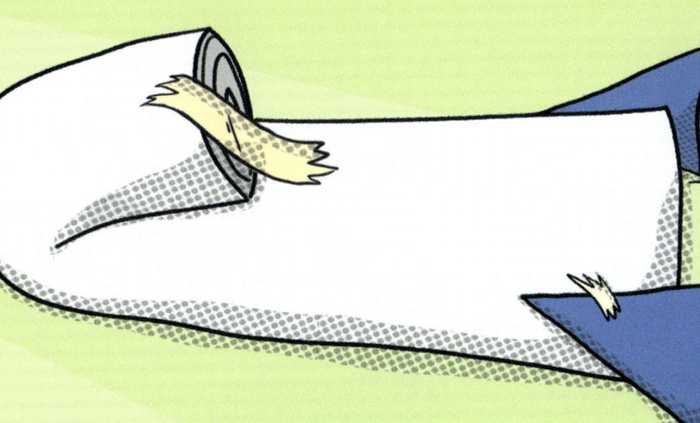

6 Slip the tube over the straw and blow hard. The tube rocket will blast off the end of the straw. Measure how far the rocket travels.

GO FARTHER

Experiment by attaching small pieces of modeling clay to the front or back to adjust your rocket's center of gravity. See if this affects how far it can fly. You could record your measurements to find the best combination. How else could you improve your rocket's aerodynamic design?

SPACE FACT

Huge spacecraft traveling through space can have their direction adjusted by puffing small jets of gas out the side of the spacecraft. The force from the jets can be very small because there is no air resistance in space to act as drag.

HURTLE TO EARTH ON AN "EGGCITING" MISSION

What goes up must come down! Astronauts return to Earth in reentry capsules that are shaped a little like an egg. Like rockets, these capsules are also designed to be aerodynamic and have a small surface area, so that they can travel quickly. They reach speeds of around 13,200 miles per hour (21,200 km/h)!

Reentry capsules have to slow down enough to land safely; otherwise, the returning astronauts could be seriously hurt. This is where drag becomes useful. Let's look at the effect of drag on the surface area of your own capsule to see how you can make it land safely!

YOU WILL NEED:

- a garbage bag
- scissors
- four 20-inch (50 cm) lengths of string
- a small plastic bag (with handles)
- two fresh eggs

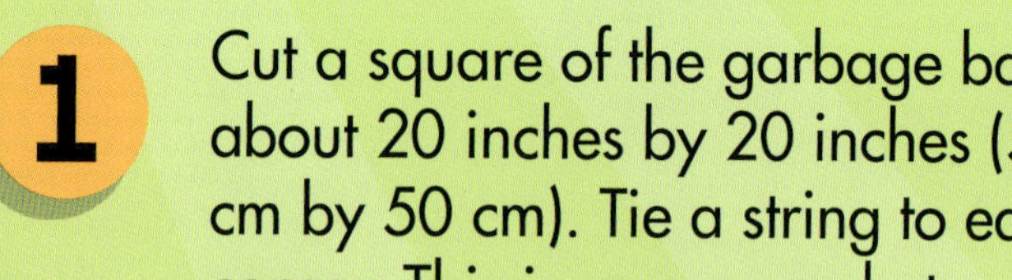

1 Cut a square of the garbage bag about 20 inches by 20 inches (50 cm by 50 cm). Tie a string to each corner. This is your parachute.

2 Tie the other ends of the strings to the handles of the smaller bag.

3 Place one of the eggs into the bag and check that it hangs securely below the parachute.

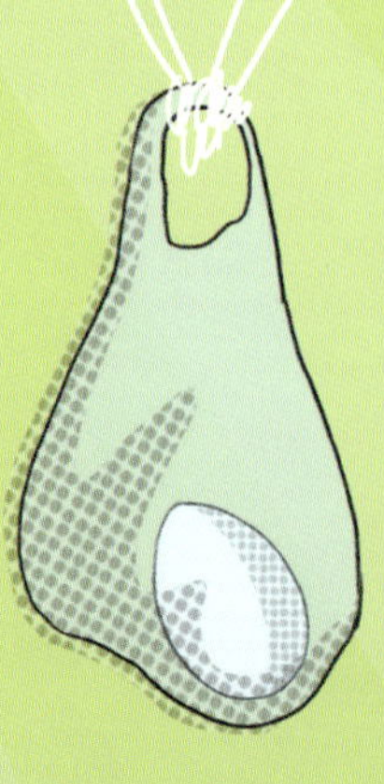

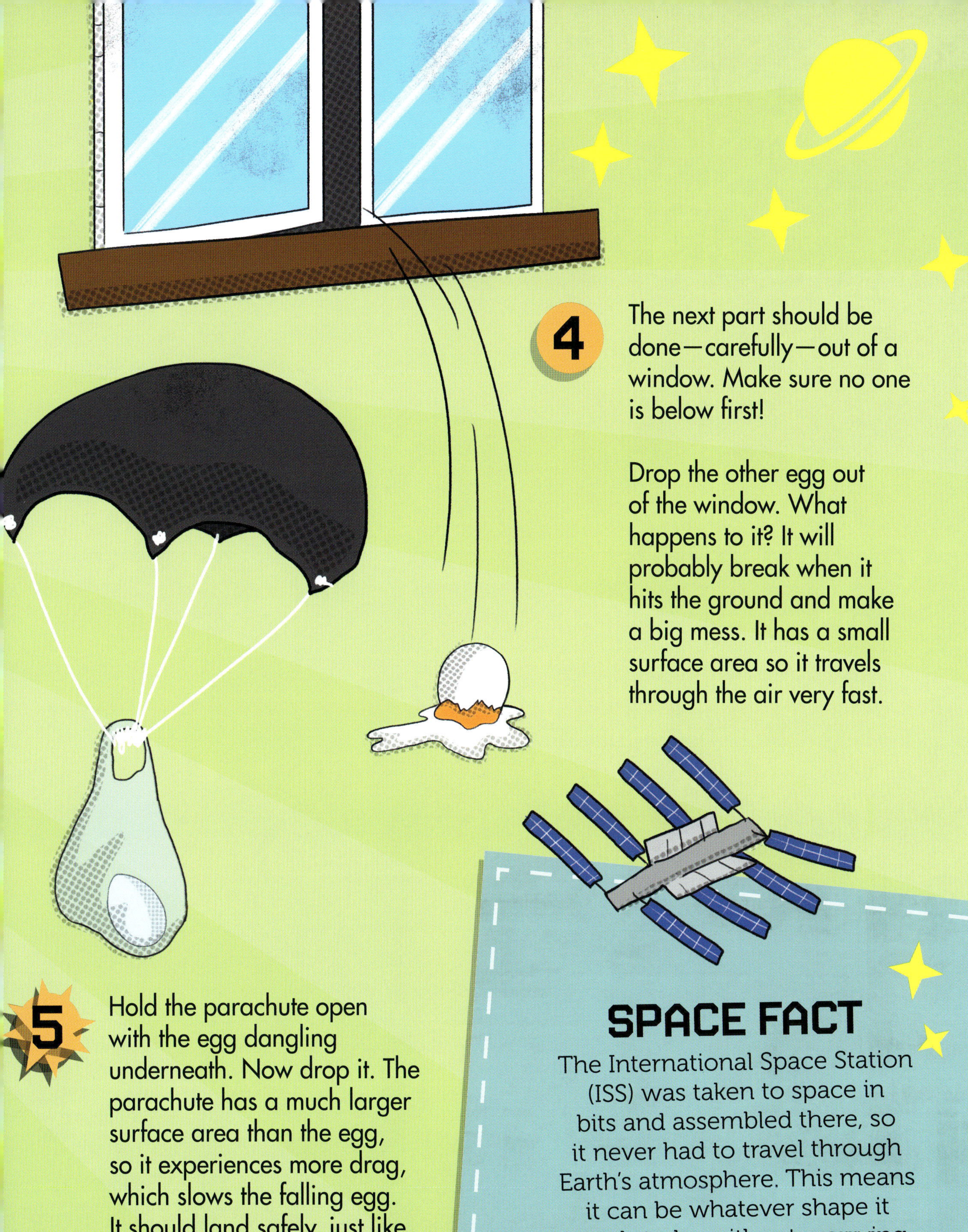

4 The next part should be done—carefully—out of a window. Make sure no one is below first!

Drop the other egg out of the window. What happens to it? It will probably break when it hits the ground and make a big mess. It has a small surface area so it travels through the air very fast.

5 Hold the parachute open with the egg dangling underneath. Now drop it. The parachute has a much larger surface area than the egg, so it experiences more drag, which slows the falling egg. It should land safely, just like a real capsule does when its parachute opens, moments before it hits the ground!

SPACE FACT

The International Space Station (ISS) was taken to space in bits and assembled there, so it never had to travel through Earth's atmosphere. This means it can be whatever shape it needs to be without worrying about drag. It isn't streamlined and instead looks like a crazy television antenna.

SEND A ROCKET INTO ORBIT

The surface of Earth is curved. In fact, Earth is just a really BIG ball of rock. When a rocket lifts off, it will usually go into orbit around Earth, where it circles in a regular and repeating path.

Earth's curve allows rockets to orbit. An object in orbit follows a curved path as gravity pulls it toward the surface of Earth, but at the same time, Earth is also curving away from it. Let's explore how orbits work.

YOU WILL NEED:

- a tennis ball
- an old pair of tights
- scissors

1. Hold the tennis ball at arm's length. Let it go and watch it drop to the floor. The force of gravity from Earth pulls on the ball so that it falls straight down.

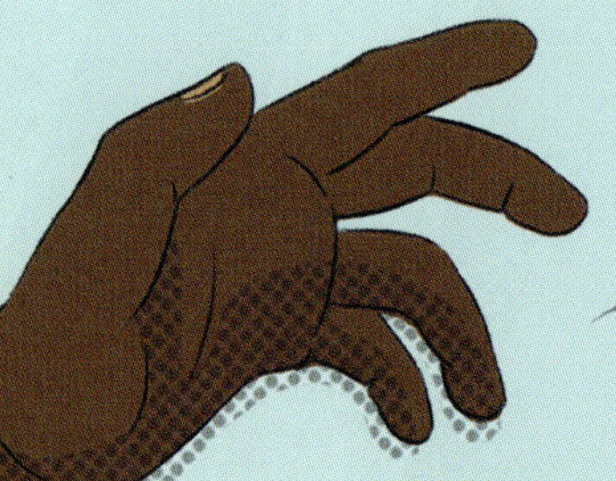

2. Now ask a friend to throw the same ball gently away from themselves horizontally. From the side, watch the path of the ball carefully and note where it lands. What do you notice? You should see that the ball follows a curved path. The ball is moving forward, but the force of gravity still pulls it down.

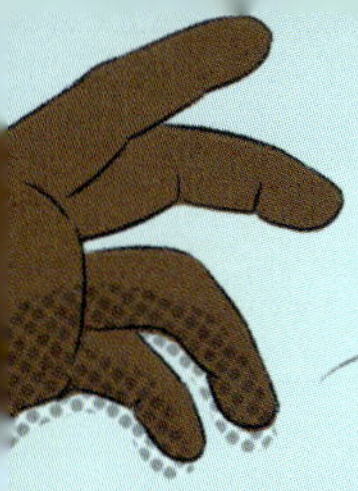

3 Ask your friend to throw the ball harder. Notice that it lands farther away but, more importantly, it follows a shallower curve before landing.

If you stood on top of the tallest mountain and threw the ball at 5 miles per second (8 km/s), the ball would follow a curved path as gravity pulls it down. That curved path would match the curve of Earth's surface. In other words, the ball would constantly fall toward Earth, but Earth would constantly fall away from the ball too. The ball would be in orbit!

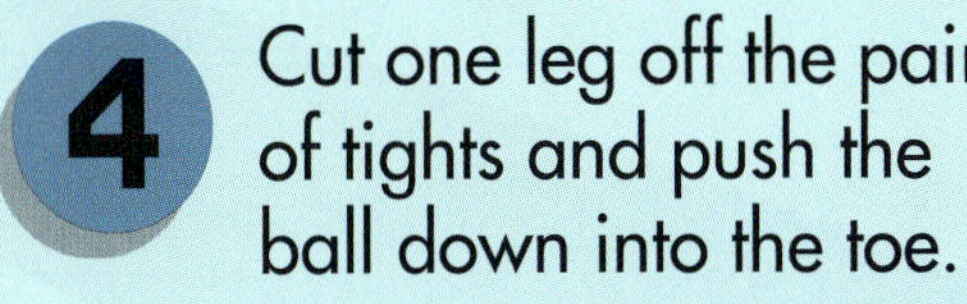

4 Cut one leg off the pair of tights and push the ball down into the toe.

5 In an open space, swing the ball in a big circle. The ball moves away from you in a straight line unless something makes it go somewhere else. (This is Isaac Newton's first law of motion.)

The force of gravity (your hand pulling on the tights) causes the ball's path to turn in a circle, orbiting your hand.

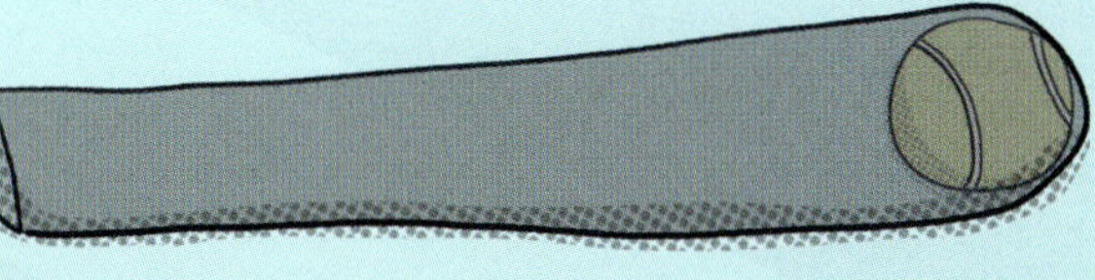

SPACE FACT

It is not only rockets traveling around Earth that are in orbit. Earth is orbited by our moon, Earth is in orbit around the sun, and the sun is in orbit around the center of our galaxy—the Milky Way.

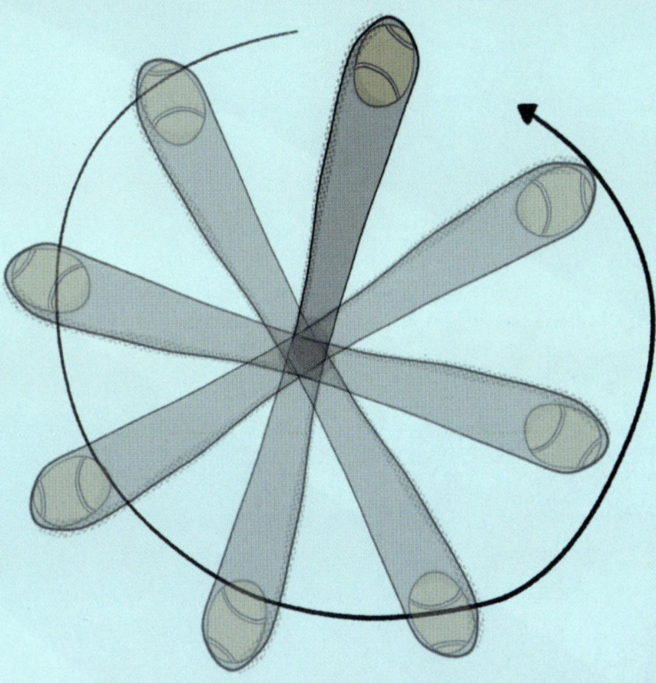

MAKE WATER WEIGHTLESS

If you watch a video of an astronaut in space, you will see them floating gently around. You might think that they have escaped the pull of Earth's gravity, but astronauts float because they are in a state known as free fall.

Objects in orbit are constantly in free fall because they are being pulled down by the gravity of whatever they are orbiting. At the same time, the object being orbited is curving away from them at the same speed (see pages 22–23). They seem weightless, because everything else around them is falling at the exact same speed. You can explore weightlessness with a cup of water, but do it outside because you might get wet!

YOU WILL NEED:

- a paper or plastic cup
- scissors
- a jug of water

1 Ask an adult to help you cut a small hole in the side of the cup. The hole should be close to the bottom of the cup.

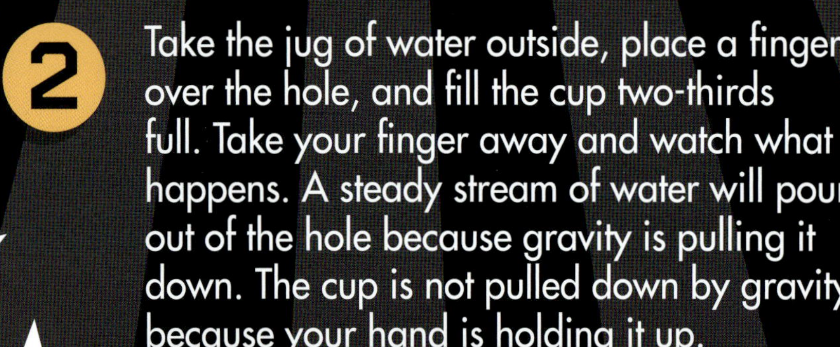

2 Take the jug of water outside, place a finger over the hole, and fill the cup two-thirds full. Take your finger away and watch what happens. A steady stream of water will pour out of the hole because gravity is pulling it down. The cup is not pulled down by gravity because your hand is holding it up.

3 Now place your finger over the hole and again fill the cup two-thirds full of water.

4 This time, gently let go of the cup as you pull your finger away from the hole. Watch carefully. Look out for the splash as the cup hits the ground!

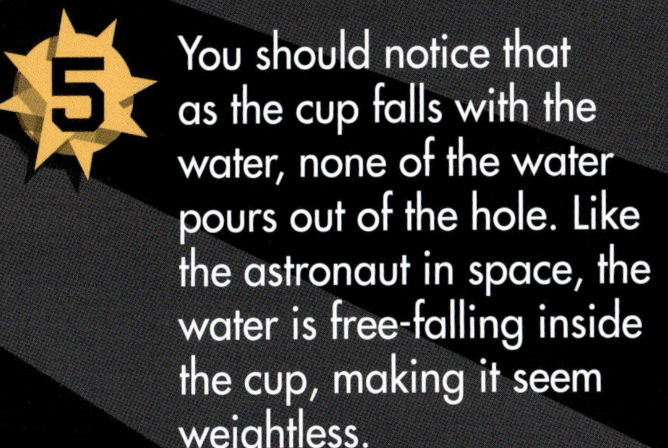

5 You should notice that as the cup falls with the water, none of the water pours out of the hole. Like the astronaut in space, the water is free-falling inside the cup, making it seem weightless.

SPACE FACT

Water in space is a very tricky thing to deal with. It is free-falling, so it is impossible to make it stay inside a cup. Instead it floats around and forms balls of water. Astronauts can have lots of fun floating around in the ISS trying to catch floating balls of water!

BECOME A ROCKET BOOSTER

Have you noticed that all space rockets have a funnel at the bottom? If you squeeze the gas from a rocket engine through the narrow part of this funnel, the gas goes through that gap faster. The speed that a rocket can zoom through space is determined by the speed the gas shoots out the bottom. Using a funnel to make the gas escape more quickly makes the rocket go even faster!

This is known as the Venturi effect and is named after the Italian scientist who discovered it—Giovanni Battista Venturi (1746–1822). You can explore the Venturi effect for yourself in this experiment.

YOU WILL NEED:

- a glass (or other container)
- some water
- a straw
- scissors
- sticky tape

1 Fill the glass with water up to about 3/4 inch (2 cm) from the top.

2 Cut the straw into two pieces. Both pieces should be about 2 inches (5 cm) in length.

3 Tape one piece of straw inside the glass: one end in the water and the other end sticking up above the rim of the glass. The straw is your funnel.

4 Take everything outside. Place the glass on a table or other surface so that you can get down low next to it. Hold the other straw horizontally, so that it is just over the open end of the funnel. You may need to experiment a bit to get this right.

5 Blow through the horizontal straw to see the Venturi effect in action! When the water (or gas out of a rocket) escapes out of the funnel, it causes the pressure in the funnel to go down. This in turn causes the water to be sucked up and sprayed out in front of you!

CREATE

You can use the Venturi effect to blow water-based paint onto a piece of paper to make cool art.

SPACE FACT

The Saturn V rockets that took the Apollo astronauts to the moon would never have got them there without the funnels boosting the speed, or thrust, of the rocket engines.

LAUNCH THE ULTIMATE ROCKET!

In the previous experiments, you have found out how to design rockets, how to use chemical reactions to push rockets into space, and even how to make rockets go faster. It is now time to build the ULTIMATE rocket! This activity is best performed outside and well away from any buildings or power lines, as your rocket might reach the height of a house!

YOU WILL NEED:

- a clean, empty 2-liter soda bottle
- a cork
- four straws (not bendy ones)
- sticky tape
- some white vinegar
- 4 teaspoons of baking soda
- paper towels

1

Make sure the cork fits the opening of the bottle. Remove the cork.

2

Tape the four straws around the neck end of the bottle. They should all stick up about 1 inch (3 cm) higher than the neck. The bottle should stand up on the straws without wobbling or falling over. Next, fill the bottle about a third full of white vinegar.

3

Put 4 teaspoons of baking soda onto a paper towel. Then roll it up, so it will fit into the neck of the bottle without the baking soda falling out. (Don't put it in the bottle yet!)

RED ALERT!

Ask an adult to help you with this experiment. It must be performed in an outside open space!

4 Now for the fun part! These next two steps need to be done quickly and you will need an adult to help you. Put the rolled up paper towel into the bottle so that it drops into the vinegar and quickly put in the cork. DO NOT lean over the rocket as you do this.

5 Quickly turn the rocket over, place it on the floor, and stand back!

GO FARTHER

Try and make your rocket go higher by fixing a cardboard nose cone to it. This will cut down the air resistance and make it go higher. You might also want to try adding some fins to the rocket too, so that it flies straighter.

SPACE FACT

When it has run out of fuel, our Ultimate Rocket falls back down to the ground and can be used again. Many rockets have parts that cannot be used again, while others have parts that fall back to Earth on parachutes and are reused.

GLOSSARY

AERODYNAMIC a shape that helps reduce the force of drag on an object

ANTACID a medicine that helps to reduce acid levels in the stomach

DRAG a force that slows down moving objects

ENGINE a machine that converts power into motion

EXOTHERMIC a chemical reaction that gives off energy, usually as heat

FORCE the pushes and pulls that cause things to move

FUNNEL a pipe with a wide end and a narrow end

GAS one of the three main states of matter. A gas can expand, squeeze, and flow from one place to another.

GRAVITY a force that tries to pull two objects together

HYDROGEN a flammable gas with no smell or color. It is a chemical element usually represented by the letter H.

MATTER stuff that makes up everything around us and is usually either a solid, a liquid, or a gas

MOLECULES the building blocks of all matter. Each molecule is made of a group of atoms.

NEWTONS the unit of measurement used for force

ORBIT a circular or oval path one object follows around another

OXYGEN a gas with no smell or color that is essential for life on Earth. It is a chemical element usually represented by the letter O.

PARACHUTE a sheet of material that fills with air as it falls, causing it to fall more slowly

PARTICLE a tiny object that makes up matter. Atoms are the smallest particles.

PRESSURE the effect of a force being applied against something

RESISTANCE an effect where something is slowed down or stopped by something else

SOLAR SYSTEM the planets, moons, and other space objects that orbit the sun

SPEED OF LIGHT maximum possible speed of any matter, which is 983,571,056 feet per second (299,792,458 m/s)

STABLE something that is not likely to wobble or fall over

UNBALANCED not of equal amounts

YEAST a microscopic fungus made of cells that can reproduce, and change sugar into alcohol and carbon dioxide

FURTHER INFORMATION

BOOKS

The Apollo 11 Moon Landing: A Day That Changed America by Amy Maranville (Capstone Press, 2022)
Explore Rockets by Lola Schaefer (Lerner Publication, 2023)
Rockets and Space Travel by Walt K. Moon (BrightPoint Press, 2023)
Superfast Rockets by Alicia Klepeis (Pogo Books, 2022)

PLACES TO VISIT

Hayden Planetarium Space Theater, New York
Kennedy Space Center, Cape Canaveral
National Air and Space Museum, Washington, DC
NASA Johnson Space Center, Houston

WEBSITES

The NASA Kids website has loads of interactive space activities, such as building your own rocket and trying your hand at driving a Martian buggy.
www.nasa.gov/kidsclub/index.html

BBC Bitesize is a great website with lots of curriculum based science activities.
www.bbc.co.uk/bitesize

The ESA Kids website has plenty of fun and games for kids to explore space.
ww.esa.int/kids/en/home

Note to parents and teachers: Every effort has been made by the publishers to ensure that the websites in this book are suitable for children, that they are of the highest educational value, and that they contain no inappropriate or offensive material. However, because of the nature of the internet, it is impossible to guarantee that the contents of these sites will not be altered. We strongly advise that internet access is supervised by a responsible adult.

INDEX